COAL

Written and illustrated by

CHARLES KING

BLACKIE
GLASGOW AND LONDON

ACKNOWLEDGEMENTS

The Author acknowledges with thanks the help given in the preparation of this book by the Public Relations Department of the National Coal Board. Thanks are also due to the Manager and Staff of Ammanford Colliery, South Wales, and to the Senior Engineering Instructor at Abernant Engineering Training Centre for technical advice and for supplying answers to myriad questions.

Printed in Great Britain by Robert MacLehose and Company Limited
Printers to the University of Glasgow

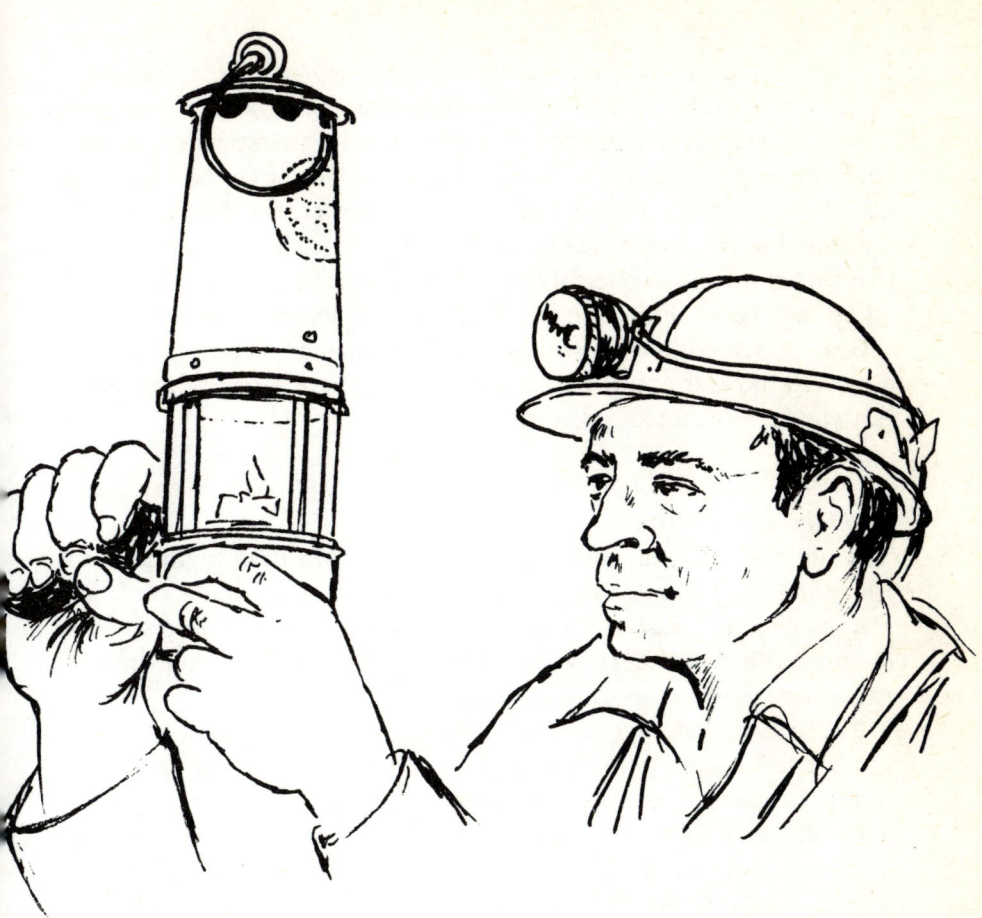

Somebody once described Britain as being 'a country built on coal and surrounded by fish'. Although fish has almost disappeared from British dinner tables (except in the form of fish fingers) for a number of reasons, there is still plenty of coal beneath the land and under the ocean floors in the vicinity of the coalfields.

There is no doubt whatever that coal is one of Great Britain's most precious assets; what is more, the coal extracted by our miners from British pits is the highest quality in the world.

In the 1950s and '60s, the feeling was gaining ground in government circles that coal as a fuel for power and industry was 'old hat', and that richer fuel prospects might be realized from heavy investment in oil and nuclear energy. Now that we have reached the '70s, it has become clear that Britain and other West European countries cannot depend upon a constant flow of cheap oil; as for nuclear energy, scientists still have a lot to learn before this wonderful form of energy reaches a state of complete safety and dependability in its use for producing power.

Coal is sometimes known as 'black diamonds' because, like the diamond, the best coal is pure carbon and both are formed deep in the earth under tremendous pressures.

The History of Coal

The story of coal is an ancient one; it goes back in time anything from 150 million to 300 million years, to the remote time when our earth was young, when its crust was still being convulsed by volcanic eruptions, mighty earthquakes and the tumblings that formed the mountains and valleys and set the shapes of the continents.

Throughout the days of this long period, the sun shone, torrential rains fell, hot, dry periods were followed by centuries of ice, which changed again to warm, humid periods. During this time plants grew, flourished and died, to be followed by their descendants over millions of years. Changes in the surface of the earth caused shifts and tumblings of the fields and forests. Fallen trees were twisted, crushed, and swallowed up by morasses and lakes. Thousands of years later, the process was repeated; new forests formed, flourished and, in their turn, were drowned and covered with silt, earth, rock and lava. As they sank lower under compression, they gradually changed their state from a woody to a carboniferous mass.

Where these coal-forming processes were interrupted by long periods of inactivity followed by further coal-formation, many layers of coal will be found today. The diagram on page 16 shows why a coal-seam might be found near or even on the surface.

The warmth-giving properties of coal were most probably discovered by early fire-making and tool-using men in various parts of the world—the so-called cavemen. When gathering fallen branches and sticks to make a fire, and stones for building a fire 'grate', many of them were no doubt surprised to find that certain black stones caught fire and provided an efficient, slow-burning source of heat. Coal had been discovered. It is easy to imagine the whole tribe rushing off to the spot where these magical black stones were found, and when all the surface lumps had been collected, eagerly digging with their stone tools to extract more and more.

One can imagine the tribe making quite a business of extracting these wonderful black stones from their territory and trading with other tribes for skins, food and clothing. One of the earliest trades in the world could well have been that of miner and coal merchant.

Traces of the use of coal in the Bronze Age have been found in Glamorgan, South Wales. In other parts of Britain the ancient Britons were using it long before the Romans came. The conquerors were no doubt glad to burn it to keep warm; evidence exists of coal stores all along the length of Hadrian's Wall.

Coal was known in ancient China; Marco Polo, friend of Kublai Khan, brought samples back to the Court in Venice, as well as pieces of a wonderful material that would not burn, even in the hottest fire—asbestos.

A National Coal Board information booklet states, 'Long before coal played its leading role in the Industrial Revolution, it was a major national concern affecting kings, nobles, freemen, merchants and labourers. Newcastle, for example, was fighting for its right to produce and profit from coal in the thirteenth century, and fighting too against its rivals north of the Border—for in Newbattle as in Newcastle, coal was a highly profitable product with its export markets both to north and south. Ships carried the coal to customers, particularly in London. By 1615, there were 400 coal-carrying sailing ships (*carbo maris*) carrying coals to London from Newcastle.'

Along with coal came a galaxy of famous inventors: men such as

Thomas Savery who developed the 'Miners' Friend' which was a steam engine that could pump water at a rate of 60 gallons a minute; Thomas Newcomen who developed the Beam Engine which was also used mainly for pumping; George Stevenson who built engines that solved the problem of pulling tubs of coal from coal-face to pit bottom, and who improved colliery railways; James Watt and Richard Trevithick built more efficient steam engines for the mining industry; William Murdoch invented the technique of extracting gas from coal; Abraham Derby invented the blast furnace; and Sir Humphry Davy one of whose contributions was to invent the miner's safety lamp that cannot ignite the methane gas (firedamp) that used to be such a danger in the mines.

The earliest coal-mines in Britain were known as 'bell pits', because they were characterized by a deep hole reaching to the coal seam which 'belled out' into a wide working chamber at the bottom. There a couple of men hacked out the coal and loaded it into buckets which were drawn up to the surface by a windlass worked by horses.

One of the great dangers in mining caves deep under the ground is falling rocks and earth. In the bell pits, men were often buried by a sudden collapse of the shaft, so a solution had to be found to prevent the recurrence of such accidents.

The answer seemed to lie in the 'Room and Pillar' mines. In these, a bell pit was excavated and squared off to form a 'room'. Another room was added next to it and another after that. The roof and the walls of the resulting honeycomb were kept up by leaving standing pillars of solid coal. This system was used for centuries, and still is, though very infrequently, nowadays. Although the coal pillars provided a measure of safety, the system came to be regarded as wasteful because *all* the coal should be extracted.

In the seventeenth century, therefore, the Longwall system came into being, in which teams of coal-cutters worked side by side at the coal-face, erecting timber supports by and behind them as they moved forward. The space behind them was filled with stone waste and spoil— 'goaf'. A single track was kept open through the waste material.

Are coal-mines always very deep? This depends upon the depth of the coal-seam. The earliest mines were perhaps no more than thirty or forty feet below the earth's surface; the coal in them has all been 'worked out'. During the seventeenth century, the Newcastle mines were at most 400 feet deep, but in the eighteenth century some mines went down as far as 1,000 feet. In the Victorian era, thanks to the power supplied by machines, some mines exceeded 2,700 feet in depth. Today, the deepest workings are about 3,600 feet below the ground.

Mining Methods
There are two methods employed in the extraction of coal—deep, and opencut or opencast. Opencast mining for clay and gravel by digging down from the surface has long been practised in this country, but it was only during World War II that coal was extensively mined in this way.

By the end of the war, coal output was about 8 million tons a year, and until 1952 the operations were controlled directly by the Government through the Ministry of Power. For some years afterwards, production was stepped up and reached a target of 14 million tons in 1958. For various reasons, the demand for coal declined, and production was held down to about 7 million tons a year. But by 1970 demand had increased so much that output from deep mining could not keep pace, so opencast production was again stepped up to fill the gap. The National Coal Board have plans to maintain opencast output at a steady 10 million tons a year; this will include a large proportion of anthracite and coking coal, both in worldwide shortage.

In the interests of the environment, no opencast site can be worked by the Coal Board without authorization from the Secretary of State for Trade and Industry. The Minister, possibly after a public inquiry, imposes stringent conditions for working and restoring the land, and the Coal Board often take the opportunity to combine pit heap reclamation schemes with opencast mining work to ensure that there is as little defacement as possible of the local landscape.

When authorization is granted, tenders are invited from civil engineering contractors. Before coaling starts, topsoil and subsoil are separately stripped and used for baffle mounds to screen the workings. The mounds are grassed, and a screen of trees may be added, if the work is carried out in a proper manner.

During coaling operations, according to the Coal Board, site roads are watered in dry weather to minimize dust, and the wheels of lorries taking coal to disposal centres are washed to prevent mud on public roads.

The large draglines used to remove overburden on many sites are

The Location of Britain's Coalfields

electrically operated and are virtually silent, and efficient silencers are fitted to other types of plant and vehicles.

After extraction is complete, the overburden, subsoil and topsoil are separately replaced to suitable contours. In other words, the site is landscaped. When restoration is complete, the land shows little evidence that coal-mining has been carried out, and it is usually sold on the open market as potential building land, unless it is intended for agricultural use.

Having had a look at the opencast method of coal extraction, we will now survey the second method—deep mining.

Coal deposits are distributed throughout the world: the most important are found in America, Australia, the Soviet Union, France, Belgium, Germany, and of course, Great Britain. There may be vast untapped sources, too, in many of the less hospitable parts of the globe, in the Arctic regions, for example, or under the wide oceans.

England, Scotland and Wales are particularly richly endowed with high-quality coal deposits. Generally speaking, there are four types of coal to be found in British coalfields: lignite, a soft coal; sub-bituminous; bituminous; and anthracite, the hardest coal.

Coalfields extend the length and breadth of Britain. Beginning with Scotland, there is the Fife, the Lothians, Douglas, Dumfriesshire, Ayrshire, Central, Clackmannan, and the Machrihanish; coming south over the Border there is the Cumberland, Canonbie, Northumberland, and Durham. All these, and those following, produce various kinds of coal, including anthracite, high- and low-volatile steam coal, and various grades of coking coal.

Further south are the coalfields of Lancashire, Yorkshire, Nottinghamshire and North Derbyshire and South Derbyshire, Leicester, North and South Staffordshire, Cannock, Shropshire, Warwickshire, and Oxfordshire, the last-named producing a high-volatile steam and household coal.

Moving westwards, until recently the Forest of Dean coalfield produced coal for general purposes; the Bristol and Somerset field yields

13

prime coking fuel. Further west, the great South Wales coal complex provides anthracite, the hardest coal of all, as well as prime coking fuels. In the South of England we have the Kent coalfield, which contains two of the most modern mines in Britain.

Although coal is one of our most valuable fuels, it has the disadvantage of creating dirt, dust, smuts and smoke. Before the enactment of certain laws, buildings in most cities were coated with black grime which corroded the stonework, damaged the lungs of the inhabitants and stunted the growth of vegetation. Nearly four hundred years ago Queen Elizabeth I was unwilling to go to London because 'she findeth herself greatly grieved and annoyed with the taste and smoke of sea coals'.

Since the Clean Air Act of 1956, conditions have greatly improved; many historic buildings such as St Paul's Cathedral have been cleaned and for the first time in centuries, they can be seen in their original glory. Moreover, thanks to the Smokeless Zone laws, they are likely to stay that way. Owners of buildings in smokeless zone areas are fined unless they use 'smokeless' fuel, material that burns cleanly without producing black smoke. Two such fuels that can be mined straight from the pit are anthracite and steam coal. Other types include coke, the first man-made smokeless solid fuel produced from coal.

Over the last few years, many man-made fuels have been developed and perfected for use in the home and in industry. These, bearing names like Homefire, Coalite, Rexco, Sunbrite and Phurnacite, are more expensive than ordinary coal but burn consistently with little ash waste.

Searching for Coal

Coal-mines do not go on for ever; pits become what is known as 'worked out', that is, all the coal that can be economically taken from the seam has been mined. All over the coal areas of Britain there are thousands of old workings from the past. These sometimes show themselves by a sudden subsidence in a field, on a road, or even among buildings. What happens when a once valuable mine ceases to yield its load of black diamonds? Nowadays, it goes without saying that a redundant mine will be closed up and made perfectly safe after removal of the machinery and equipment.

The obvious answer is to search for new seams deep under the ground. How is this done? This is where the geologist comes in. His studies of the underground formations of a particular locality enable him to say, 'Trial borings should be carried out at this place because geological evidence leads us to expect to find a coal-seam of considerable magnitude.'

A derrick is set up, and a special power-driven drill bores into the ground; samples of the strata, the size and shape of apple cores, are brought to the surface from various levels. A rock drill is used first for penetrating the shallower strata, then the harder diamond drill is used to obtain the cores.

These cores give the geologist a picture of the rock formations beneath the rig. Mud and water is pumped through the centre of the drill rig; this lubricates the hardened steel cutting 'bit' at the bottom. The mud returns to the surface, bringing with it the debris of the drilling. If coal is found, further samples taken at increasing depths will prove whether the seam is a workable proposition. If it is, a shaft or inclined drift is sunk from the surface. When required, a series of radiating underground tunnels will be cut.

Undersea coalfields form an important part of our coal reserves. Here too, the geologist's skills are employed. To obtain accurate knowledge about the structure of these undersea areas, and to learn about the position and quality of the seams, a sea boring tower is used. A recent search off the Durham coast proved the existence of at least 550 million tons of workable coal in seams lying under the North Sea. This particular rig worked in about 100 feet of water and drilled bore-holes nearly half a mile into the seabed. In addition to the drilling of bore-holes, National Coal Board geophysicists have conducted seismic and other surveys in areas where the water was too deep to use the boring towers.

Building a New Mine
Building a new colliery is a big project costing millions of pounds. How is it done? We have noted how the search for new coal supplies begins

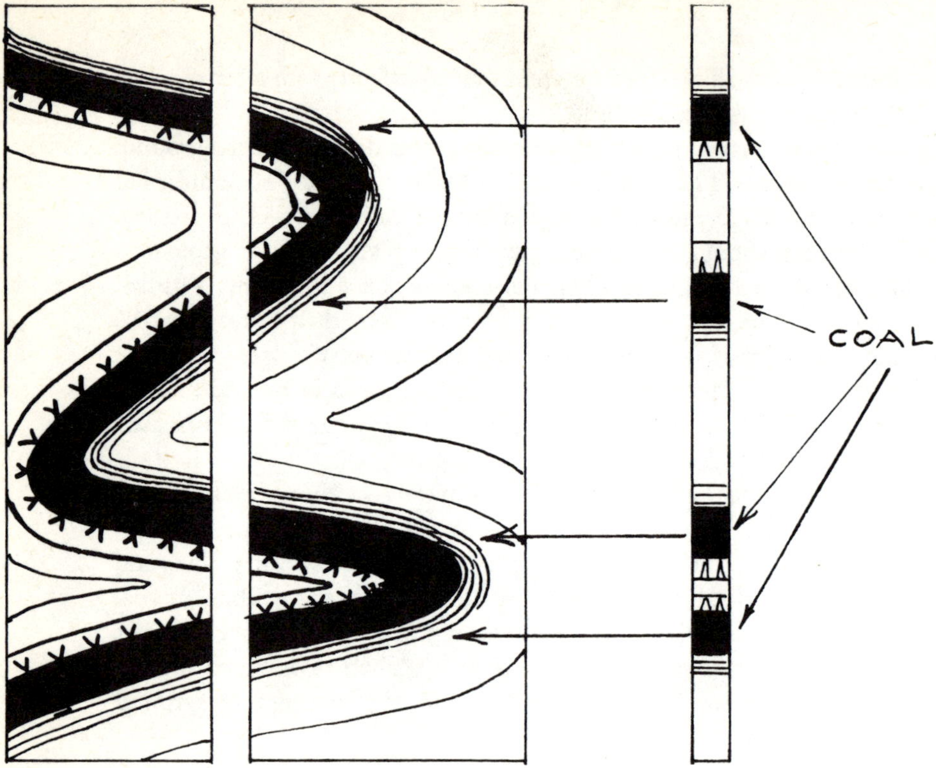

COAL

(A)

(B)

Bores and Cores Diagram (A) shows a coal seam folded back on itself due to pressures and movements in the earth's crust. (B) shows the core extracted by the boring equipment. It looks like four different seams, but (C) the geologist can tell that the tops and bottoms of the seams have changed places

(C)

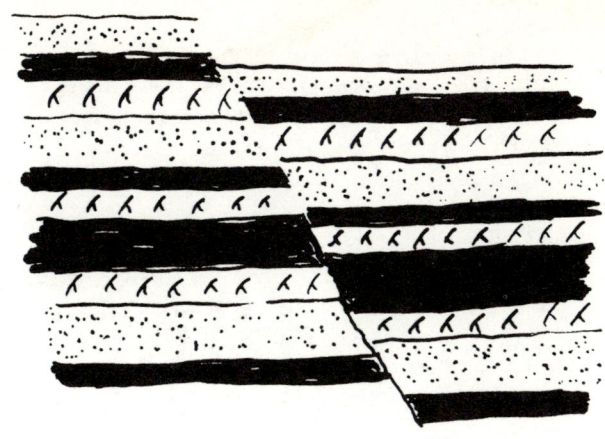

A Typical Fault   The miner finds that the seam he is working on is suddenly cut off at the fault; on the other side, it lies at a higher or lower level

with the geologist, but what happens when he has succeeded in finding a rich seam?

The first step is to sink two shafts. These are made by digging a huge well, and lining it with concrete or bricks. The shaft sinkers ride to the bottom in a big bucket or 'hoppit' which is also used for carrying the rock they excavate to the surface. Quite often on a job like this, the ground is wet and porous, and if certain steps are not taken, the shaft would soon turn into a water well. To prevent this, before sinking begins, freezing pipes are embedded in the water-bearing rock to create a solid wall of ice to keep out the water.

When the shafts have reached the required depths, a network of tunnels is driven on a horizontal plane according to the master plan. This work is done by using explosives and excavating machinery.

The tunnel plans include a ventilation system of air-lock doors, fly-overs and air-regulators so that, eventually, every part of the new mine will be ventilated. A vast amount of equipment has to be moved into position underground. They include items like rails for the diesel engines, the engines and trains themselves, steel arches for roof supports, hundreds of thousands of bricks to line the tunnels, fire-fighting equipment, complete workshops of maintenance gear and tools, coal-cutting

FIRST STEPS IN SINKING A SHAFT.

The shaft is started with the aid of diggers, a crane, and a large bucket called a hoppit. The earth is loaded into the hoppit and pulled to the surface

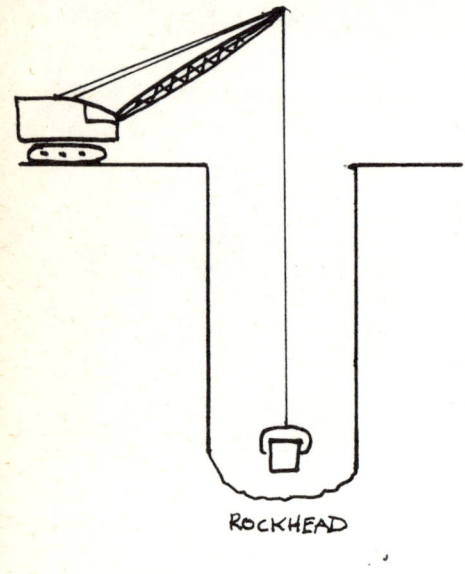

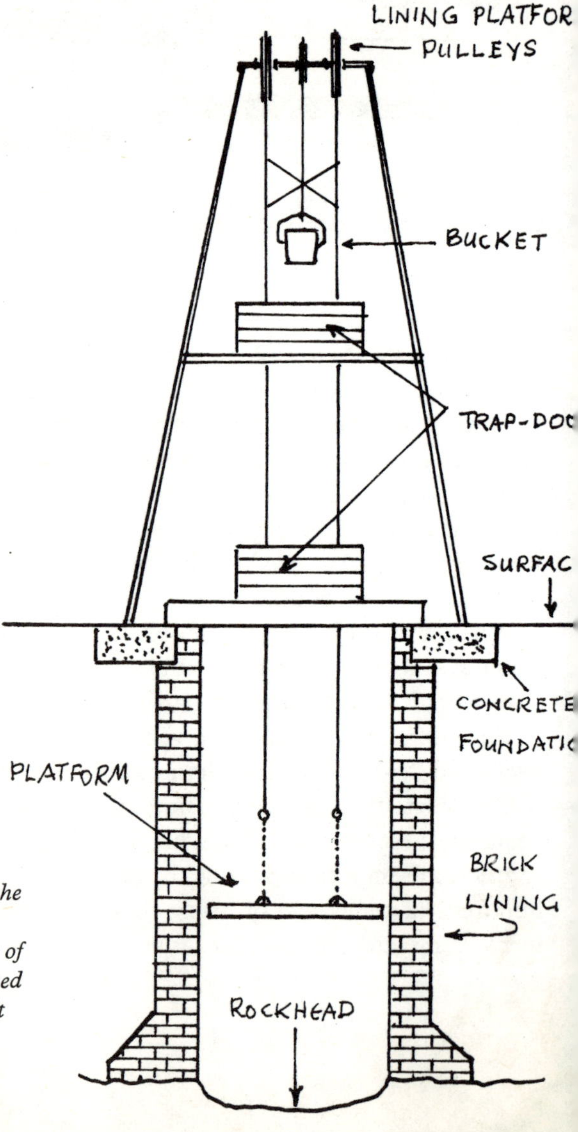

ROCKHEAD

LINING PLATFOR
PULLEYS

BUCKET

TRAP-DO

SURFAC

CONCRETE
FOUNDATIO

BRICK
LINING

PLATFORM

ROCKHEAD

The brickwork lining for the shaft is built from the bottom up on the strong rockhead. The heavy headgear can then be erected without the danger of the shaft sides collapsing. A winding engine is used to raise the broken rock in the hoppit as the shaft becomes deeper machines and conveyors. In fact, everything for running a coal-mine is taken down the shafts.

On the surface, the mine's power-house has to be built, headgear installed, stores and workshops established, and a thousand other important items of building and equipment organized. If it is like one of the new mines in Nottingham, situated in pleasant countryside, it may well have its own housing estate for the mine-workers with shops and a sports centre.

At Lea Hall colliery in Staffordshire, two 24-foot diameter shafts were sunk to a depth of 1,200 feet, passing through 640 feet of water-bearing sandstone which had to be frozen before the shafts could be sunk. This mine is worked on two levels, and about 30,000 yards of underground roadway were built. The full range of surface buildings include a Coal Preparation Plant and a conveyor system to take coal direct to the power station nearby.

Shirebrook Colliery, North Derbyshire, is an example of a major mine reconstruction. One of the shafts has been deepened by 750 feet, new underground roadways and new transport systems installed and all equipment electrified. Surface buildings, including the Washery, have been replaced. As a result of the £4 million 'face-lift', Shirebrook has been completely transformed above and below ground. Old miners who worked in the original colliery, sunk in the nineteenth century, would not recognize it today.

Inside a Coal-mine

What is it like to work in one of Britain's modern coal-mines? Are all coal-mines situated in dismal industrial areas? Does the scenery consist of ugly towering slag-heaps and rows of grim grey houses? Certainly, slag-heaps exist, unfortunately, but there are plans to level and land-scape them, which will bring the land into use again, but this is a long-term job. Many old coal-mining areas are grim and depressing; but many of the new ones are situated in pleasant rolling countryside, and one would hardly realize that such a basic thing as a coal-mine existed in such a spot.

This giant roadheader, looking like something out of science fiction, is the latest method of driving new 'roadways'. It is quicker and safer than conventional shot-firing. Its head, armed with banks of cutting teeth, can be directed at any angle and is electro-hydraulically driven

Only the two tall headgears, with their spinning pulley wheels, indicate that it is a colliery, and that men are busy mining coal more than a thousand feet below. Other structures are neat and low and so designed that they do not intrude.

By 1974, there were about 275 collieries in Great Britain, and they are each different. However, they all have one thing in common: they rip the coal from the seams, bring it to the surface, sort and clean it, and despatch it to the places where it is required for turning into the power needed for industrial and domestic use.

Let us have a look at a modern colliery and see what goes on. We arrive and are met by the colliery manager who conducts us to his office. He explains that the organization and working of a modern pit is extremely complicated. The colliery manager is responsible for the safety of his men, the smooth running of the pit, and for the maximum production of the coal.

This colliery is a well-designed complex. Once the miners arrive at the colliery and go through a door near the canteen, they remain under cover until they reach the cage that will take them down to the workings.

A Sea Boring Tower

Near by are the locker rooms where the men change into their working gear; next to these are the pithead baths. In the early days of mining, workers used to go home taking the dirt and coal-dust with them on their clothes, strip off, and have a bath in a tin bath in front of the fire. Today, of course, every pit has its pithead baths, locker rooms, canteen, medical centre and welfare officer.

Beyond the baths is the lamp room, where the miners collect the electric lamps which are the only source of light for them on the coal-face. Then there is an underground passageway which leads to the cages that take the men down the shaft. This and another shaft are the only means of communication between the open air and the coal-face. These cages convey all the men and equipment, and bring all the coal up.

The shafts carry the vital fresh air down to the workings. They also carry water pipes and the power cables which take electricity from the surface to the workings, which may be as far as two miles from the bottom of the shafts.

The manager points out a large three-storey building. This is the Coal Preparation Plant, nicknamed the 'Washery', where the coal is sorted by size, cleaned of impurities, and then loaded into wagons which are marshalled on the nearby sidings into trains that take the coal to consumers all over the country.

We are given a guide and taken to the locker room, where we change into some old clothes and overalls for our visit to the coal-face. We are handed a leather belt, a light-weight safety helmet, a pair of tough boots with steel toecaps, a pair of leather knee-pads and a pair of thick leather gloves.

We follow the guide to the lamp room, where rows of batteries are stored in racks equipped with battery chargers which automatically re-charge the lamps. The heavy battery clips on to our belt, and the lamp, attached to a stout flex, clips on to the front of the helmet. Ready to go, it is hard to suppress the slight feeling of nervousness at the prospect of going down several thousand feet into the bowels of the earth.

The manager approaches—'Did you remember to take off your wrist watch?' In fact we *had* forgotten to take it off in the locker room when we deposited matches, lighters and cigarettes in the steel locker. A watch can easily be damaged or get coal-dust in the works, so he takes charge of it.

Our guide carries a Davy safety lamp; this is used to test for the presence of dangerous gases underground. This is done by examining the flame, which looks different in the presence of gas. Miners are taught how to 'read' the flame.

Forward now down the long passage to the cage, accompanied by miners going on their shift. Just before we reach the cage, a man frisks us for contraband—cigarettes or matches. Should a man be so foolish as to conceal such items, or be criminally stupid enough to strike a light underground, he could cause an explosion that could kill or maim all his comrades. Every precaution is taken against the possibility of fire or an underground explosion. All electrical equipment is so protected that there is no chance of a spark causing an explosion of mine gas.

About twenty of us enter the cage in charge of a man at the surface called the 'banksman'. He signals to the 'winding engine man' that the cage is ready to go, but before it moves, he must wait for a similar signal from the 'onsetter' who is stationed at the bottom of the shaft. At first, the cage drops gently, but it gathers speed as we drop down to pit bottom. In the pitch darkness, the only light comes from our helmet lamps. Dropping at this speed the strange feeling of weightlessness makes you wonder if the contraption has got out of control, but the other chaps do not seem to be worried, and it is not long before the cage decelerates and comes gently to a stop.

The cage gates open into a long, well-lit tunnel stretching into the distance. Other tunnels branch off and lead to diesel locomotive repair shops, and stores full of mining equipment. We climb into a train of open cars drawn by a diesel locomotive, and begin our mile-and-a-half journey to the coal-face.

The brightly-lit tunnel is lined with bricks supported by steel arches. When the train stops, we alight and start to walk. Soon, the only lights are those on our helmets, and the tunnel becomes narrower and rougher. We bang our heads on the low, rock roof and are glad of our helmets.

We have reached the end of the journey—we are at the coal-face. Faced with a frighteningly narrow hole, about three feet by two, we hesitate. Our guide gives us an encouraging smile as if to say, 'After you, sir.' He indicates that if we wish to see how our miners earn their bread, we must crawl into that dark hole and wriggle like worms along the rocky way among the hydraulic pit-props for a hundred yards. We know now why we were issued the knee-pads and gloves!

As coal-dust fills one's mouth, one begins to regret taking on this assignment, but there's no turning back now. Except for the bobbing lights of the miners' headlamps there the darkness is Stygian. We become suddenly and acutely aware of the millions of tons of rock and earth above. But nobody else seems to care much that we have only about three feet headroom. Here, in this dark cavern, is the trepanner, the coal-cutting machine, and a forest of hydraulic props surmounted by thick, rigid bars keeping the roof up.

The team have crawled through into the coal-face and the machine starts up. The din is terrible! The steel-clawed giant plunges forward, biting huge chunks out of the 200-yard-long face. The armoured conveyor, a mighty steel chain enclosed in a metal frame, clanks along like an armoured tank. Somewhere ahead it sounds as though a gang of demons are playing 'war' with pneumatic drills. The noise is indescribable. As the team bellow remarks to each other through the din, and we see their white teeth gleaming from their black faces, an awesome respect for them grows—they do this every day for a living.

Although water sprinklers play on the conveyor to keep down the dust, they fight a losing battle; at the pithead, on the surface, huge fans draw the foul air up the 'upcast' shaft, which helps keep the atmosphere in the workings as clear as is possible. A constant breeze blows through the system; this draught carries away the all-pervading dust and also prevents the accumulation of harmful gases. At the surface, clean, fresh air is drawn down the 'downcast' shaft and is circulated throughout the mine by the powerful ventilation fans.

Included in the ventilation lay-out is a system of air-lock doors which regulate and adjust the amount of air flowing through the tunnels; there

are also 'fly-over' junctions where an intake and a return airway cross one another.

Sitting among the forest of props, it is hard to see exactly what is going on, but we gather that the trepanner with its whirling head of picks is relentlessly working its way forward into the coal-face and throwing its harvest onto the conveyor which carries it to the far end of the coal-face. Loose lumps of coal on the floor are shovelled on to the conveyor.

The conveyor itself is moved closer to the face by hydraulic rams which are also used to move the roof supports forward. The pitprops supporting the roof are built like hydraulic jacks. As soon as the trepanner has passed by, every second prop is moved in to support the newly-formed roof. The conveyor is rammed forward so that it is in the right position for the next cut. When it is ready, the other props are moved forward to the new position. The old roof, now unsupported behind the props, is allowed to fall in.

These mining aids 'walk'—all the miner has to do is to turn a valve to control the oil-operated 'Pushers' which move the conveyor and advance the props. This makes it possible for two men to look after a 180-yard-long coal-face.

What happens to the stream of coal hacked out by the trepanner? From the armoured conveyor it is discharged on to a belt conveyor which carries it to the pit bottom. This coal joins another stream coming from a different direction on its belt; the double torrent is tumbled down a spiral chute into a huge bunker which holds 600 tons. From here it is fed into skips which carry ten tons at a time up the shaft, where it eventually finds its way to the washery.

A Forest of Pitprops   *A miner moving powered supports forward by push-button control at the coal-face. The only light comes from his cap-lamp and those of his mates*

The whirling teeth of the trepanner bite into the coal-face. In its wake, the armoured conveyor is rammed forward close to the face as other men in the team move the hydraulic roof supports forward to support the newly-exposed roof

HOW POWERED SUPPORTS WORK

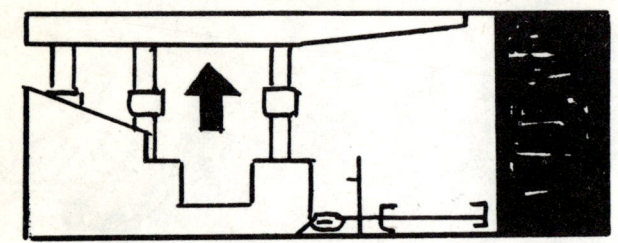

(*A*) *Vertical supports are extended to bring the roof beam into contact with the newly-exposed roof*

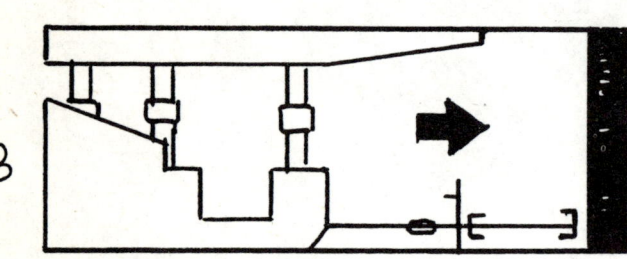

(*B*) *The power-loader passes on the loading run, the double-acting ram extends and pushes the conveyor forward*

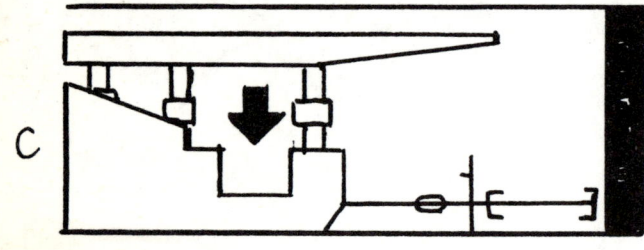

(*C*) *Vertical supports are lowered*

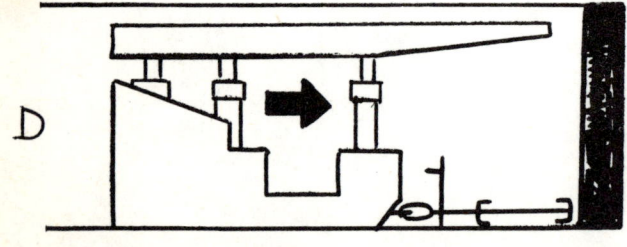

(*D*) *The ram is set into reverse and the support is drawn up to the new face-line. It is then re-set to the roof, as in (A)*

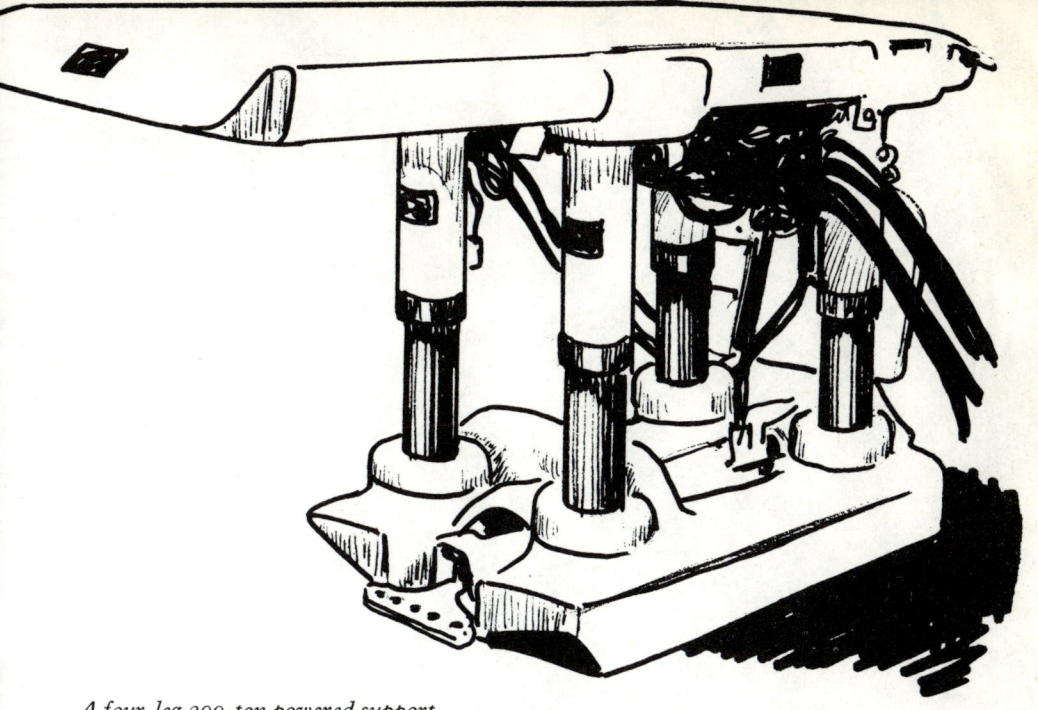

A four-leg 200-ton powered support

After crawling and stooping our way along the coal-face back to the place we entered, it is a great relief to be able to stand upright and stretch.

As we make our way towards the spot where we pick up the little train, the never-ending stream of coal flows along beside us on its trunk conveyor to its final destination.

It is sometimes necessary to use explosives to blast away the rock in order to extend the workings at the coal-face. Men called 'shot firers' carry out this task; after drilling one or two holes in the rock, they insert sticks of a special kind of dynamite. Everyone takes cover when the electrically-fired charge brings down about 20 tons of rocks and dust. This noxiously unpleasant episode—fumes from the explosive, the whirling dust, and roaring noise—is yet another common part of a miner's shift.

After seeing all there is to see at the coal-face, it is time to make our way to the other shaft that will take us to the surface. We enter the cage,

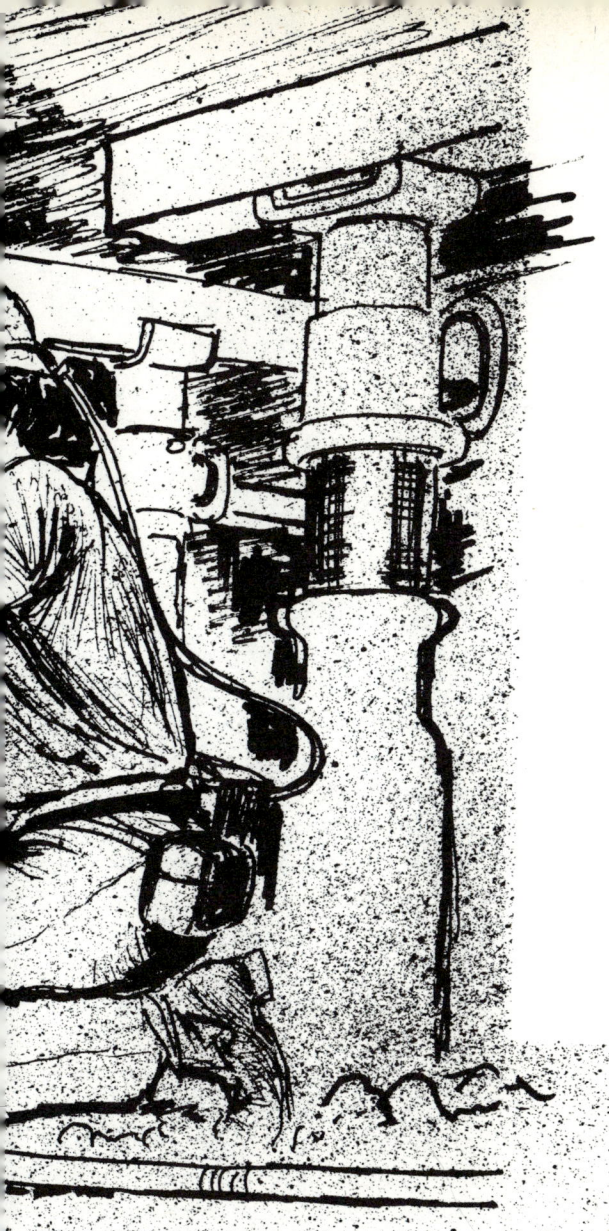

Shot-firers use a power-drill before placing their explosive charges to extend the roadway. Charges are laid in a certain pattern to obtain the maximum effect with the minimum amount of explosives. The smoke and dust caused by the explosion will be cleared by the mine's ventilation system the onsetter giving his signal that people and not materials are aboard, and we shoot upwards. No feeling of weightlessness this time—just the opposite, as our feet feel impacted into the steel deck of the cage.

Into the locker rooms to dump our dirty clothes; now for a welcome hot shower to remove the coal-dust from eyes, nose, ears and hair, and a brisk rub-down afterwards. Dressed in our own outdoor clothes, we go to the canteen to swallow many cups of tea to wash the coal-dust from our throats. The adventure is over, all loose ends tied up, even to the extent of retrieving our matches, lighters, cigarettes, and the wrist watches.

What happens in that three-storey building we mentioned—the Coal Preparation Plant? Streams of coal arrive here by underground tunnels. Dirt, rock and shale are removed from the coal before it is loaded into the railway wagons.

Huge, powerful magnets remove metallic debris, and the coal passes through great steel riddles or sieves which grade it into various sizes for passing through the plant. The noise of the shaking screens assaults the ears like gunfire. The coal is graded into three sizes: very large, medium and small. The large lumps are sorted by hand by three men on a circular 'picking table'. Lumps containing shale and stone are rejected; the smaller stuff is passed through special washing baths which separate the coal from any impurities. After this, the 'clean' coal goes to other screens where it is again sorted to size for customers' requirements.

New Mining Technology
In a pamphlet issued by the National Coal Board, the following statements appear: 'Powerful coal-cutting machines, automatically steered along the coal-face by a radio-isotope, mine up to five tons a minute from the seam. . . . Strategically located tubes breathe in the mine air around the clock for instant analysis, to give early warning of any contamination. . . . Coal is simultaneously weighed as it is carried out of the mine on a conveyor travelling at 750 feet a minute, and in seconds, it is X-rayed for ash content . . . the specified coal is ready for burning—in a revolutionary room-heater which 'eats' its own smoke and provides

the cheapest central heating of all fuels. . . . This may read like a science fiction account of how coal can be mined and used by the next generation.'

This is all scientific fact *now*, says the Board. The nucleonic steering devices have been tested on thirteen underground power loading machines; automatic mine air sampling is installed at forty collieries, and will be extended to them all.

At Longannet in Scotland, coal from a complex of four linked collieries is weighed as it travels on a $5\frac{1}{2}$-mile-long computer-controlled conveyor, while Lynemouth Colliery in Northumberland is one of twenty-six pits which can use instant X-ray equipment for measuring the ash content of coal.

All this is certainly a long way from the old pick-and-shovel days, but let us take a closer look and see what it all means to the young recruit entering the mining industry.

Item number one—why the radio-isotope steering device? Nucleonic steering of power loaders prevents expensive coal-face machines from cutting stone from the roof or floor of the coal-seam. Gamma rays 'measure' the thickness of the coal and control automatic steering equipment which keeps the machine's operating horizon within the seam. The value to the Coal Board is increased output with greatly improved consistency of quality, giving coal of lower ash content and better roof conditions in the seam.

A great deal of research has resulted in the improved design and mechanics of power loaders and cutting picks. In the past, many picks were attached to the fast-spinning drum; today, fewer and larger picks, turning at lower cutting speeds, produce much more of the valuable large coal and create less dust in so doing. Trials using water for keeping down the dust at the face show that water is used most effectively at the cutting point.

Item number two—the 'breathing tubes'—is especially interesting. In the old days, miners had to rely on smell or the presence of mist and condensation to detect underground heatings, that is, spontaneous combustion in parts of the coal-seam. Today, new techniques give early warning of those gases such as carbon monoxide, hydrogen sulphide and the oxides of nitrogen, which, like carbon dioxide, are the products of combustion.

The NCB pamphlet quotes the remarks of a colliery manager at one of the forty collieries where continuous night and day mine air sampling automatically takes place: 'Now, for the first time, I can go home at the weekend without wondering what may be happening at the pit.' Adequate ventilation, supported by constant sampling of the air in the mine, provides the first line of defence against explosive and poisonous gases.

28 ft-LONG CUTTER-LOADER

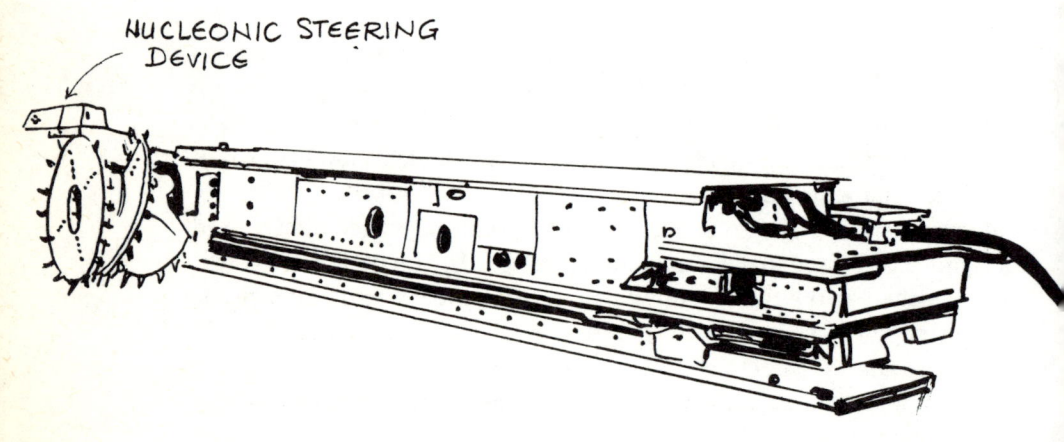

NUCLEONIC STEERING DEVICE

Some pits give off large quantities of methane gas. In the old days, this would be a constant source of danger, but nowadays the gas is piped from its source in the coal strata to the pithead where it is used to fire the pit's boilers or sold to industrial customers.

At ordinary pit temperatures, coal produces carbon monoxide in tiny, but measurable, quantities. As the temperature rises, hydrogen is produced; ethylene and propylene are produced at still higher temperatures. This phenomenon makes it possible to detect the beginning

150 H. P. RANGING SHEARER
AND THE TYPE OF CUT IT
MAKES.

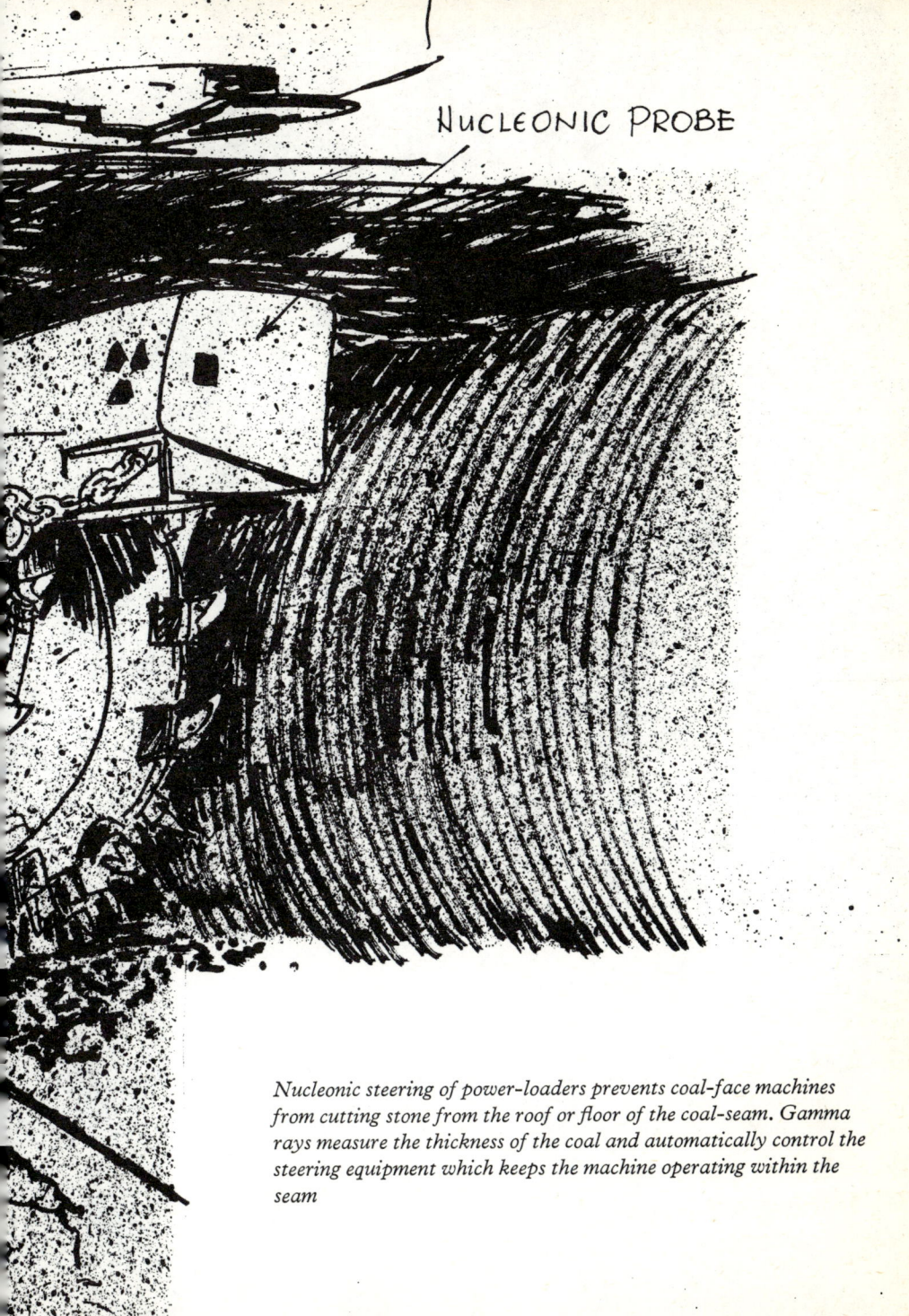

NUCLEONIC PROBE

Nucleonic steering of power-loaders prevents coal-face machines from cutting stone from the roof or floor of the coal-seam. Gamma rays measure the thickness of the coal and automatically control the steering equipment which keeps the machine operating within the seam

WATER SPRAY AT CUTTING POINT

Double-ended ranging drum shearer   The water spray at the cutting point lessens the dust at source. This machine is operated by remote-control equipment by the machine operator

of hotting-up, to monitor the success of efforts to suppress hotting-up, and to measure the temperature of the coal.

The appearance of ethylene, for example, would indicate a coal temperature of at least 100°C and that the position is becoming critical. But for all practical purposes, carbon monoxide is still an effective watchdog, provided it can be harnessed.

This is done either by instruments placed underground which transmit the information received to the surface, or by physically taking the mine atmosphere to the surface through bundles of tubes. These narrow tubes (a dozen in a bundle measures only $1\frac{1}{4}''$ in diameter), which can be up to four miles long, are run off from junction boxes to the separate 'districts' to 'breathe in' the mine air. Samples from each district flow continuously to the surface and are automatically monitored for gases by infra-red absorption and other techniques.

Another weapon in the armoury against mine gases is the light-weight 'self-rescuer' clipped to the belt of every miner. This is a kind of gas-mask, and its purpose is to enable men to pass safely through carbon monoxide concentrations which follow an explosion. Each self-rescuer is examined monthly for damage, and is weighed to find out if the filter has picked up moisture to an extent which might affect its performance. If any set has picked up between 4 and 10 grammes of moisture, it is sent to the laboratory for regeneration.

The third item of interest—X-raying coal for its ash content—concerns selling coal by grading methods. While the coal is passing through the pneumatic coal-carrying systems, X-ray and radio-isotope monitors check the ash content in seconds. The instruments measure electro-magnetic radiations which reveal the mineral content of the coal, and hence its ash.

In many collieries miners may have more than a mile-long walk from the cage at the pit bottom to their coal-face, but in the more modern pits, diesel locomotives hauling man-riding cars take the men along illuminated tunnel 'roadways'.

The use of sophisticated lighting on the coal-face itself has finally engaged the attention of Coal Board engineers, and in the last four years

Miner wearing the 'self-rescuer' His nose is pinched by a spring clip and he draws air in through the mouth. This apparatus gives the wearer protection from carbon monoxide for at least an hour. It must always be kept free of moisture which could make the chemical in the bag useless

thirty coal-faces have been fitted with brilliant tube lighting. The NCB have realized that when men are able to see team-mates and obstacles as much as 50 yards away, there is less risk of accidents, as materials and equipment can be a danger in the inky darkness.

Naturally, this move has won applause from the miners who spend their working days at the face, lit only by their cap-lamps.

An Old-fashioned Colliery

After all these modern wonders, it will be an interesting change to look at a really old-fashioned colliery, one built in 1895, but still producing about 2,500 tons of fine anthracite each week. Situated at Rydaman (Ammanford), South Wales, all the coal-getting at this colliery is done with pick and shovel—the miners call it 'stealing' the coal, because of the natural geological difficulties. 'Things are easy for the miners up in Yorkshire and Derby,' the men told me; 'the seams lie lovely and

43

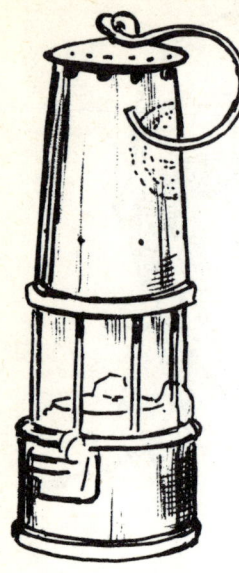

Testing for Firedamp   What the miner sees when firedamp or methane gas is present. (A) shows the flame adjusted for testing. At 1¼ per cent of gas, the flame grows (B), at 2 per cent the flame takes the shape of a pyramid (C), at 3 per cent the pyramid grows taller (D), and at 4 per cent the flame has become a cone (E). The miner's flame lamp is still the simplest and most common instrument used in testing for firedamp. When gas is present, a bluish spire forms above the normal flame

THE MESSAGE OF THE FLAMES

A   B   C   D   E

Testing Flame   1¼ PERCENT   2 PERCENT   3 PERCENT   4 PERCENT

A miner taking a sample of mine air with a Garforth bulb near a shot-hole. He will inject the sample into a special socket in his flame lamp

flat and level, while in this pit, and in other Welsh mines, the strata wriggle up and down like snakes.'

The premises are nearly eighty years old, and they look it, but all the amenities are there—medical centre, pithead baths, canteen, welfare office, and a branch office of the miners' union, the NUM. This little colliery does not have the usual two shafts; it is what is known as a drift mine. Two tunnels descend at an angle of about 30 degrees: down the first, the miners go to the face in man-carrying trolleys; from the other, the coal is drawn up in small iron wagons, each holding about 25 cwt of anthracite, by steel cables powered by electric motors. Fourteen wagons hitched to each other come up to the surface about every half hour. The combined load of 18 tons is run along to a cage where a surface worker tips them upside down one by one. The rich black harvest falls down a chute into the waiting lorries below. As the colliery does not have a washery, the coal is taken to the preparation plant at the modern Abernant complex, seven miles miles away.

Here at Ammanford Colliery, there are no such luxuries as 'walking pitprops'; the pitprops are all of the old-fashioned kind—finished pine logs of 6″ diameter, which lie heaped in their thousands, together with other heaps of ash baulks about 3′ 6″ by 6″ square.

At this colliery, they test for firedamp (methane gas) with the flame safety lamps instead of using the modern tube-probe method. Air samples are collected in a rubber bulb and injected into the lamp through a ring around the wick. The presence of firedamp can be 'read' by the manager, his deputies, shotfirers or any team leader, and the method is perfectly safe and efficient.

Explosives are stored in a brick building standing somewhat apart. As we enter, the typical, sweet smell of gelignite pervades the air. Our guide opens cupboards along a long wall in which are stored various kinds of blasting material: 'Dynafrax' is in sticks 8″ long, and wrapped in chrome-yellow waxed paper; the gelignite is similar but thinner. Bundles of fuses are kept in brown paper bags; these are 2″-long bright-copper-coloured cylinders with thin, covered wires attached.

In another building, we go through a turnstile into the lamp room; there we see the charging racks for the batteries that the miners carry for their cap-lamps, rows of self-rescuers and, in the office, the flame safety lamps.

What about ventilation at this colliery? Our guide asks if we would like to see where the miners go to their work, and leads us to a brick building. We hear a loud humming sound. 'Hold on to your hat!' he says, as he opens the first of two air-lock doors. Inside, it is inky black, and the noise grows louder. He opens the second door after closing the first, and the noise and blast hits us—a solid wall of stale, black, dust-laden air. The 500-hp fan is working full blast, and we have to shout to hear each other.

Facing us is a muddy tunnel which slopes suddenly downwards at 30 degrees; the pitch black is punctured every 20 feet or so by feeble electric lights. We walk down through the gale on steps laid almost a century ago, next to the rails for the man-carrying trucks. The steps are slushy with soft black mud. We wonder, if it's like this only 100 yards from the surface, what can it be like below? Our guide tells us that the men work in seams only 3 feet high, so it is pick and shovel work on their knees for 7 or 8 hours, less the break for coal-dust-flavoured beef sandwiches and a drink of cold tea. Unlike other old mines, they do have a conveyor into which they load their 'stealings'. We are reminded that this is an old mine due to be run down; eventually, these seams will be incorporated into another colliery. The men will hand in their picks and shovels—the older ones will retire while the younger men will do their stealing in brighter, healthier conditions with modern equipment.

Hard and dangerous work? Certainly. In 1973, ninety miners were killed in British pits, and thousands of others sustained injuries ranging from minor to near-fatal. On the other hand, many miners survive long into retirement—doing their football pools or tending their racing pigeons.

We ask our guide, 'What about the men who form the rescue teams during mining disasters, and how does the system work?'. He tells us that there are permanent centres where the teams work shift systems around the clock. They can be rushed to any district in their area. Their vigorous life is filled with activity and hard training. They are constantly learning new methods of life-saving and rescue in varying conditions.

We wonder out loud, 'Supposing that luckily their services are not called on for a long time. Wouldn't they get stale and bored with all that waiting?' He stares at us, his eyes wide open.

'My goodness,' he says, 'those chaps lead a heck of a life! They're kept hard at it all the time, training, training, training, just in case they get soft. Those fellows are fighting fit, and need to be!'

Becoming a Miner

Nobody could call the work of a miner's job soft; it is dirty, it can be dangerous, and in relation to other jobs, wages are low. It takes a real man to become a miner at the coal-face, and several qualities are needed —physical fitness, a good deal of pluck, loyalty to one's team-mates, skill, and at certain times, a touch of heroism.

Conditions of work are improving, even if somewhat slowly, but this

47

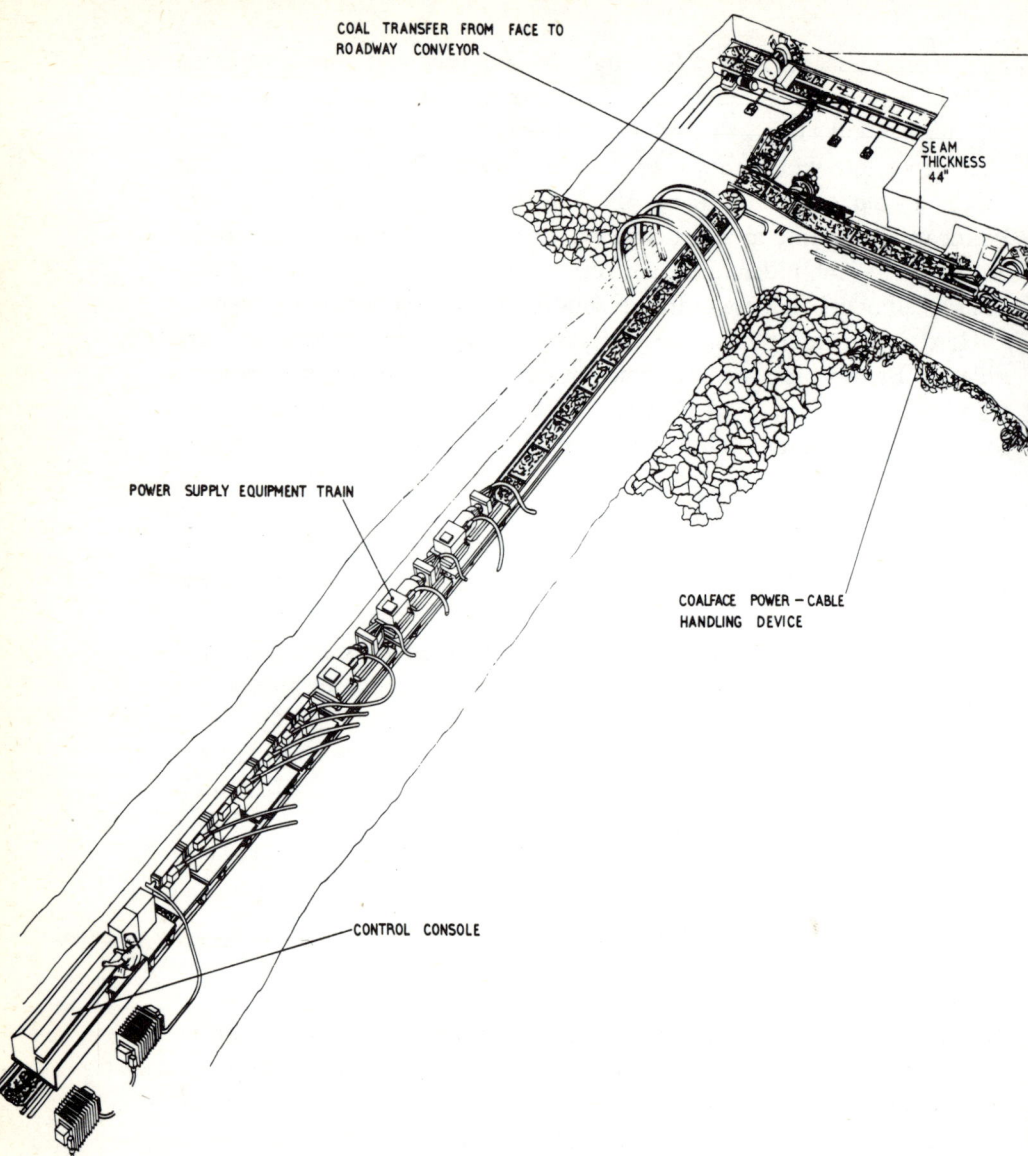

COAL TRANSFER FROM FACE TO
ROADWAY CONVEYOR

SEAM
THICKNESS
44"

POWER SUPPLY EQUIPMENT TRAIN

COALFACE POWER – CABLE
HANDLING DEVICE

CONTROL CONSOLE

48

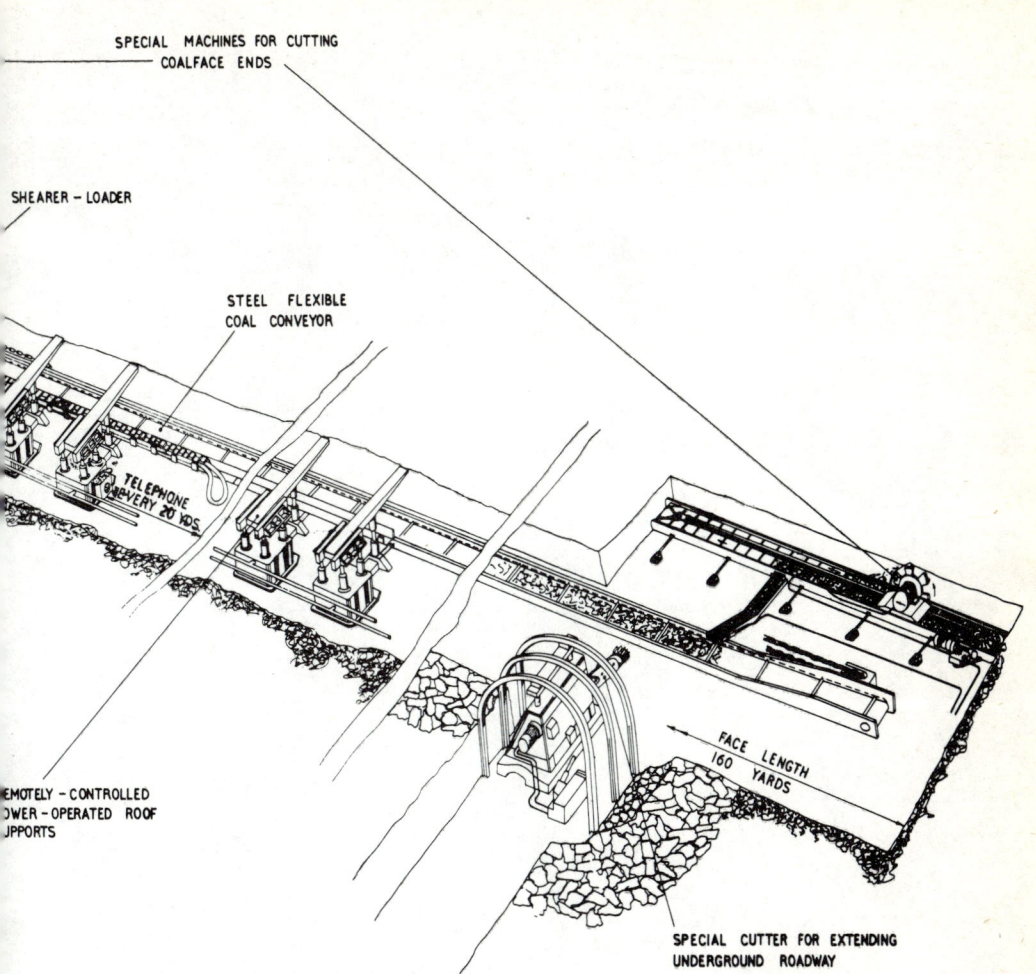

SPECIAL MACHINES FOR CUTTING COALFACE ENDS

SHEARER – LOADER

STEEL FLEXIBLE COAL CONVEYOR

TELEPHONE EVERY 20 YDS.

REMOTELY – CONTROLLED POWER – OPERATED ROOF SUPPORTS

FACE LENGTH 160 YARDS

SPECIAL CUTTER FOR EXTENDING UNDERGROUND ROADWAY

ROLF (Remotely Operated Longwall Face) diagram reprinted by courtesy of the National Coal Board. Remote control of coal-face operations was first tried at Bowburn Colliery in 1956; two pilot projects at Newstead and Ormonde Collieries followed. Someone pushes a button, and deep under the ground the machines start to work, cutting the coal, and delivering it to the Preparation Plant. The complex is operated from a control room on the surface

49

can take place up to a certain point, as coal can only be won in the end by hand. The Coal Board have been experimenting for several years with 'pushbutton mining', where machines only are used at the coal-face. The idea is to push a button and deep under the earth the machines cut and convey the coal to the Preparation Plant—no men at the face, only machines. The name for this project is ROLF—Remotely Operated Longwall Face.

Much of the modern equipment we have already discussed went to support the idea—the 'walking' pitprops, the automatic steering system which uses the radio-active probe to measure the thickness of the seam, and the automatic shearers and trepanners.

All this is a far cry from the mining methods of a few years ago, when, to get the coal, miners used explosives to burst open the coal-face, then used pick and shovel to hack out the coal and load it on to the trolleys and depended on the old-fashioned pitprops to support the walls and roof. Many miners worked at the face in gangs without the safeguards of gas-monitoring equipment and self-rescuers, and without amenities such as pithead baths and medical centres.

Today, a job in mining is a good job with a future; indeed, even as these pages are being written, the Coal Board have indicated that in the near future they will need 30,000 more men to enter the industry. Not all these men will be face workers—the skills of the electrician, engineer and fitter are needed to maintain the mines in tip-top running order.

What about shift-working? Doesn't working at odd hours upset a young man's social life? The answer to that one is this—many jobs involve shift-work: the Police, Hospital and Ambulance work, the Armed Services, the Fire Brigade, public and private services transporting people and goods, and so on. In fact, *all* the vital services that need to be maintained to keep our country running.

All the collieries in Britain work a five-day week on a 24-hour basis; that is to say, a man might work a couple of weeks on the night shift, then change over to the early morning one, and then again will come another change of work time. No young man worth his salt minds too much about giving up a bit of social life, and there is great compensation in the friendliness and team spirit that exist among colliery workers. On Saturdays and Sundays the maintenance men take over, to service the mighty coal-cutting machines, the electrical and hydraulic systems, and to ensure that in general the pit is ready and safe for the coming week's work.

Coal-mining, like many other trades, has its occupational diseases. The disease most likely to be contracted by the coal-miner is the one known as anthracosis, the form of pneumonoconiosis peculiar to coal-miners. This is caused by the inhalation of fine particles of coal-dust. It leads to the development of fibrous tissue in the lungs, permanently dilates the fine bronchi and lung tissue and increases any tendency to emphysema.

Modern, efficiently ventilated mines minimize the risk at source by carrying away the rock and coal-dust from the workings. Water-spraying at the cutting points and over the conveyors (the source of most of the dust), combined with regular medical examinations also help in combating this health hazard. Cases of anthracosis are becoming far less common as a result, but when they do occur, the sufferers can be given a change of occupation early enough to arrest development of the disease.

It might be thought that if miners were issued with a kind of gas-mask (or dust-mask), the danger of contracting anthracosis would be lessened, but this is not practical. Mining coal is heavy work, and as anybody who has had to wear a protective mask knows, it is extremely uncomfortable during violent activity or sustained strenuous movement. The answer for those engaged in trades which produce dust of any kind, whether it be from grain-handling, wool and linen spinning, quarrying or cement working, is efficient ventilation of the premises to carry away dust-laden air.

There are four main training schemes open to school-leavers. For boys who want to become skilled mineworkers, the **Mine Training Scheme** is completed in under twelve months with the opportunity of coal-face training at about the age of 18. The **Mining Craft Apprenticeship Scheme** prepares entrants for supervisory or specialist posts. The **Engineering Craft Apprenticeship Scheme** trains fitters, electricians and other craftsmen, and finally the **Student Apprenticeship Schemes** provide training in mining, electrical or mechanical engineering for school leavers with certain educational qualifications. Full details of these schemes will be gladly supplied by the National Coal Board, Hobart House, Grosvenor Place, London, SW1. The interested reader can also consult his school Careers Officer, his local Careers Officer at the Youth Employment Service, or any NCB office if he lives in a mining area.

Lack of space forbids a complete run-down on prospects and training on all four schemes, but here is a brief review of one of them—the **Engineering Craft Apprenticeship Scheme.**

In the modern apprenticeships of the National Coal Board, nothing is left to chance. Each apprentice follows a carefully planned programme of instruction designed to give him a thorough grounding in his chosen trade. This programme is drawn up for him by training staff who will keep in close touch with him throughout his training.

New methods of training have made it possible to reduce the length of apprenticeship to four years. Training normally begins with a course of full-time instruction in the basic skills of the trade. This is followed by planned practical experience at collieries and workshops; instruction on mining machinery and equipment is given by qualified instructors at NCB Engineering Training Centres. Day release to attend a technical college is also included in the programme and boys are encouraged to take craft qualifications; some will go on to qualify as Colliery Engineers.

The apprentice's training is checked at every stage, and after four years, apprentices should qualify for skilled work and a craftsman's rate of pay. Those who obtain the necessary technical qualifications stand a good chance of promotion to supervisory posts after experience as craftsmen.

Who can apply? If you are under seventeen, or in certain cases a little older, you may be considered for a Mechanical or Electrical Craft Apprenticeship. You stand a good chance if you are intelligent, physically fit, and keenly interested in engineering. Apprenticeship works in two ways. The NCB undertake to train you to be a competent craftsman. You, in your turn, will be expected to use the opportunities provided. This will not stop you leaving the industry during your apprenticeship, but if you complete it, you will be a skilled man with an assured future in mining. When you apply for such an apprenticeship, you will be asked to say whether you are more interested in the electrical or mechanical branch of engineering, and if you are granted an apprenticeship it will normally be in the branch of your choice. You can apply to change over at any time during the first two years if you find your interests lie more in the other branch. You may also apply for transfer to the Mining Apprenticeship Scheme which, if you are accepted, will prepare you for more senior posts.

Apprenticeships are awarded after the applicants have been interviewed by a selection panel. If you are selected for an interview, you will be invited to appear before the panel at a Coal Board office in your area. This panel will consist of NCB officials, a Trades Union representative, and in some cases, someone from the local Education Authority.

During the first year you will be thoroughly instructed in the use of hand and machine tools. This is taught either at an NCB Training Centre or technical college. In many areas, boys attend a technical college full time, with full pay, for three terms. In each of the remaining three years, you will be given a 20-day course on the maintenance of mining machinery at one of the Board's Engineering Training Centres. Your progress is assessed by practical and written tests.

You will also get practical instruction working with skilled craftsmen in surface workshops and underground. This will cover all the principal types of mechanical (or electrical) equipment in use at the collieries. Some time may also be spent in engineering and drawing offices.

Boys are granted day release to attend a technical college one full day per week (on full pay) to pursue courses of technical education. These courses lead to Class II and Class I Certificates of the Mining Qualifications Board, which a boy will require if he aims to become a supervisor. Normally apprentices start on the City and Guilds Colliery Mechanic's (or Electrician's) Craft Certificate, or the corresponding Certificate of the Regional Examining Union.

However, if you have done well at school, you may take the General Course in Mining, leading to a Technician or an Ordinary National Certificate Course. In addition to your day release, you may have to attend evening classes one or two evenings per week.

Regarding holidays, you will get the usual annual holiday with pay;

you will also get paid for the statutory holidays each year—Bank Holidays for example. In addition you will get seven 'rest days' a year with pay. Wages are fixed from time to time by agreements between the Board and the National Union of Mineworkers. If, during your apprenticeship, you have to live away from home temporarily, to get some special training, you will get travelling expenses and lodging allowances. You will be provided with such hand tools as you may need for your training during working hours, but if you wish to acquire your own tools you may buy them from the Board at cost price. What other benefits are offered? After you have worked for the Board for a year you have the benefits of the NCB Sick Pay Scheme. This means that you can get the Board's Sick Pay, in addition to National Health Sickness Benefit if you have to stay away from work for some time through illness. When you work for the Board you also join the Mineworkers' Pension Scheme; you pay a part of the cost of building up funds for a pension when you retire—the Board pay a much greater part. If you marry or have to look after a household, you will probably get an allowance of coal either free or at a greatly reduced price.

A complete Training Establishment for Mining and Engineering Craft apprentices is incorporated in the big modern colliery complex at Abernant. In the National Coal Board's West Wales area alone, over 700 young men are currently engaged in learning what mining is all about. At this training centre, facilities include a huge workshop containing lathes and other engineering equipment, hydraulic (walking) pitprops, stripped-down shearers, electric motors, and examples of the other kinds of machinery used in the mines of today.

The courses run for four years, and school-leavers are welcome. As well as being taught the practical and technical sides of mining, the boys learn discipline and self-reliance; at these schools too, comradeship and trust are inculcated into the young men, because if such virtues are needed anywhere, it is in mining. Apprentices are well paid, and paid holidays total 24 days in each year; there is also assisted travel.

As might be expected, all the boys at Abernant, about fifty of them, are pretty husky types, enjoying a game of rugby in their spare time.

The NCB realize the value of team games and do all they can to encourage sport and healthy pastimes. In the spacious, well-appointed classrooms, the apprentices were quiet and attentive, for they were preparing for the NCB examinations. These exams can lead to top jobs in the field of Mining Engineering, and the boys are free to study in the Board's time.

In the workshop, small groups were in the charge of white-coated instructors, who were teaching them the mysteries of the walking props with their built-in hydraulic rams which, when a face is sheared, move forward at a touch of a lever so that the mighty machines can rip another skin of coal from the face while the roof remains safely supported. Another group of boys was learning how to replace a certain valve in the working parts of a shearer which is also hydraulically driven.

More and more young men are needed to work and maintain the exciting new machinery that has been installed in Britain's modern collieries, and many good chances are open to those who want to obtain first-class jobs. Nobody could call modern mining a dull industry—it offers a challenge to anyone with the will to get on.

Coal By-products

This is really a larger subject than coal production itself. Throughout the nineteenth century and the first half of the present century, the gas industry relied entirely on coal as its raw material and produced coke as a by-product. One of the most important uses of coal is to make coke, which is used in blast furnaces to make iron. The iron and steel industry depends on a good supply of strong, high-quality coke which is made by heating selected coal in 'coke ovens'.

Modern coke ovens are immense and complicated plants, but the principle on which they work is very simple. In the following amusing experiment, you can make a simple coke oven from a clay tobacco pipe. Fill the bowl with pulverized coking coal and seal the top with a piece of clay or plasticine. When the bowl of the pipe is heated the coal gives off gas. This is like ordinary household gas, and can be lit at the mouth-

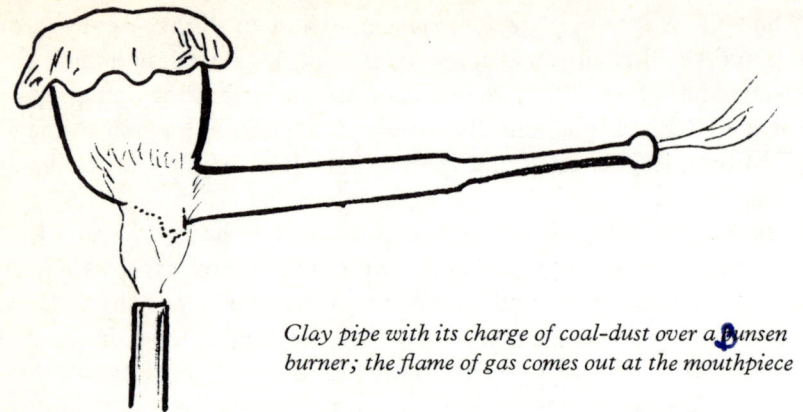

Clay pipe with its charge of coal-dust over a Bunsen burner; the flame of gas comes out at the mouthpiece

piece. When all the gas has been consumed, the flame will die out. Remove the clay seal, and the bowl will be found to contain coke.

In the old days, domestic customers always took a few bags of coke with their coal deliveries; it was cheap and thus helped to ease the families' fuel bills, but it is difficult to light in an open fire.

By-products of coal made by the chemical industry comprise a fantastic range: dyes, drugs, explosives, flavourings, perfume, paints, plastics, and man-made fibres are derived from coal-tar; ammonia, asphalt, among other waterproofing materials, and coal gas are produced from the same process.

It is obvious that many of our everyday necessities and conveniences would not exist without coal by-products.

At the present time, there is a world-wide shortage of the best coking coals, traditionally needed to make the right grades of coke which are essential for blast furnaces at iron and steel works and cupolas at foundries. Faced with this problem, British scientists have come up with an answer by perfecting a range of 'factory-made' cokes.

In blending plants, selected coals and coke 'breeze', itself a by-product, are blended with 10 per cent or less of scarce prime coking grades to make the new coke; the key to successful blend preparation is consistent proportioning of each component.

With the discovery of big reserves of natural gas under the North Sea, the gas industry no longer requires large quantities of coal, and less and less of it will be used for making gas until it is phased out altogether. With it will go gas coke, used widely in industry and in the home, especially in smoke-control areas.

This has meant that the Coal Board has lost a valuable customer, but the problem is levelling itself out. Good coking coal is in short supply, as we have noted, and the NCB is ready to supply industry with its new blended product. With the Gas Boards switching over almost entirely to off-shore natural gas supplies, there were fears at the NCB that the coke oven gas would have to be flared off—wasting a valuable natural asset and losing a valuable market for the coal industry. However, many large new customers have been won, including steelworks, glassworks, chemical works, and big users like trading estates and hospitals, for coke oven gas which is piped direct to them.

Coal for Power

Coal, the faithful fuel you can depend on, has come into its own again. As a result of the uncertainty in the supply of oil, coal has a brighter future than ever. The Americans announced in 1974 that they will be spending 10,000 million dollars (about £4,000 million) on coal research over a five-year period; the NCB has budgeted £4 million. The Coal Board will need recruits to run the new collieries, and to replace men retiring from the industry.

Most of the electricity generated in Britain comes from the energy stored in coal.

It is a common belief that power station boilers burn lumps of coal straight from the coal trucks. In fact, the boilers use pulverized coal. Lumps of coal are ground to dust in the pulverizer and blown by a current of air into the furnace where it is consumed. Special dust-catchers remove the 'fly ash' produced by the burnt coal-dust and prevent it from getting out of the power station chimney.

The furnace is designed to use *all* of the heat given out by the coal as it produces steam (and to let as little as possible escape up the

59

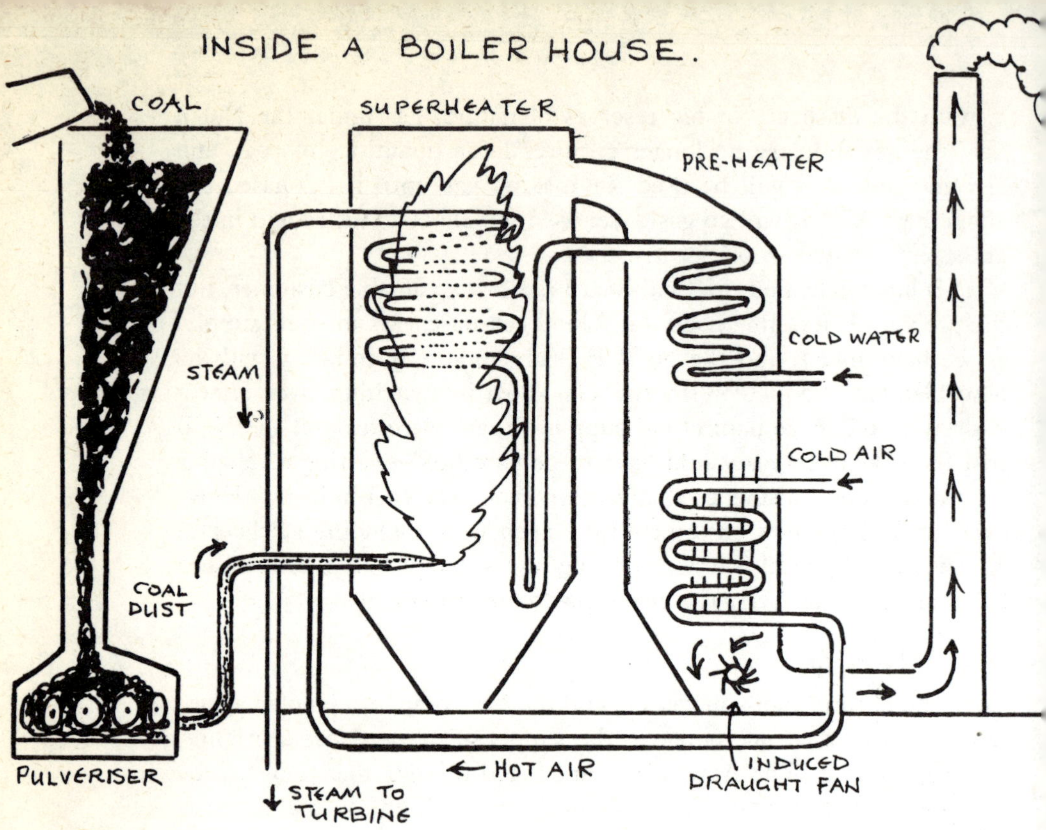

INSIDE A BOILER HOUSE.

COAL

SUPERHEATER

PRE-HEATER

STEAM

COLD WATER

COLD AIR

COAL
DUST

PULVERISER

↓ STEAM TO
TURBINE

← HOT AIR

INDUCED
DRAUGHT FAN

How pulverized coal is turned into the electrical power which drives the turbines and generators which in their turn provide us with light, heat, and power for our homes and industries

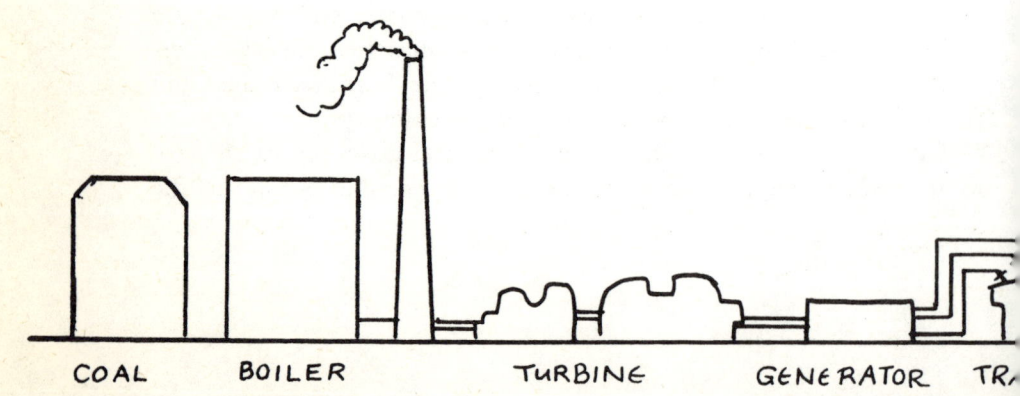

COAL   BOILER   TURBINE   GENERATOR TRA

chimney). The furnace is surrounded by boiler tubes which are filled with water to produce steam; this steam is made still hotter by passing it through the tubes of the 'superheater' at the top of the furnace.

The 'red-hot' steam goes from there to the turbines. The hot flue gases (which would normally escape through a chimney) are used first to heat the water fed into the boiler tubes, and then to heat the air in which the coal-dust is burned in the furnace.

The energy of the steam is converted into mechanical energy in the turbine. The steam is contained under high pressure and directed at the windmill-like blades of the turbine. The conversion takes place in a number of stages, through a series of turbine blades. Each ring of moving blades alternates with a set of fixed blades which redirects the steam on to the following set of moving ones. As the steam must expand through the turbine, each set of blades must be a little larger than the preceding one, to accommodate the greater volume of steam.

The condenser changes the low-pressure, fully-expanded steam back into water ready to be returned to the boiler. The condenser which lies beneath the turbine is cooled by a continuous stream of cold water pumped through tubes. The cooling water absorbs heat in the process, and, in many power stations, is diverted to huge concrete cooling towers to dissipate the heat.

The turbine driving the generator works on the same principle as the simple bicycle dynamo. Because of the size, the generator produces a lot of heat. In some modern stations, the generators are fitted with coils made of copper tubing, instead of wire; this makes it possible to cool the generator by pumping cold water through the coils.

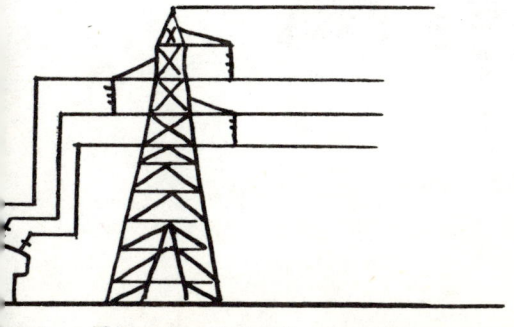

ER TRANSMITTING LINES *from NCB diagrams*

The potential energy of coal is thus finally changed to electrical energy and transmitted from the power stations to the national grid.

This energy drives our trains, lights our homes, schools, offices and factories, powers our industrial complexes and many other facilities, including radio and television. And the source? The coal from the mines that lie deep in the seams under many regions of the British Isles.

This coal is our native, natural asset; it is priceless, indispensable, yet there were many in the 1950s and '60s who believed that coal had had its day, and that oil and atomic energy would be the exclusive fuels of the future. The rise in the cost of imported fossil fuels has made us realize the importance of using the home product, and coal has come into its own again.

A Headgear